PRESENT
BETTER THAN
STEVE JOBS

SECRETS TO A PERFECT PRESENTATION...
FROM SOMEONE WHO ACTUALLY DOES IT

DAN LIER

Human Behavior Expert and International Speaker

PRESENT BETTER THAN STEVE JOBS
Dan Lier
Human Behavior Expert and International Speaker

Copyright © 2013 by Dan Lier

All rights reserved. No part of this book may be used or reproduced in any manner whatsoever without written permission, except in the case of brief quotations embodied in critical articles or reviews. Please do not participate in or encourage the piracy of copyrighted materials in violation of the author's rights. Purchase only authorized editions.

CONTENTS

Introduction 1

1. Most of Us are Not Celebrities 5
2. The Unfair Advantage 9
3. Psychology 17
4. Pre-Game 21
5. The Five Steps to a Perfect Presentation 25
6. The Connection 29
7. Agenda 41
8. Your Message 47
9. Review 59
10. Inspire To Action 63
11. Building Your Skills 67

About the Author 79

INTRODUCTION

Being in the game of public speaking for over 20 years, I've seen and heard it all. When I say "I've seen and heard it all," I'm saying those words with 100 percent certainty.

I've seen "no-name" speakers who are "off the charts" fantastic. I've seen big-name celebrity speakers who were just awful. I've seen big-time authors or TV personalities speak for a corporate group who couldn't adjust and connect to the audience and fall flat on their face. I've seen mediocre corporate speakers who are magical in their connection, so likeable and warm, yet not bringing any value.

Becoming a great public speaker or presenter is not an easy proposition. Speaking in public and delivering a solid message is a "skill-based" art form, and I'm passionate about helping people who have the desire to raise their skill levels. I've been coaching people on speaking and presentation skills through my Speakers Academies for over 12 years, whether being hired by companies to improve their sales or leadership teams or hired individually by those who are committed to excel. People not only grow with confidence when they learn the proper fundamentals and raise their effectiveness at delivering a message, they also advance in their careers. Having the ability to deliver a message in a public speaking format is a separator. It separates the great communicators from the amateurs.

Like anything else, to be great you must have the proper fundamentals. Speaking is an art form, yet it's skill-based art. If a person starts with incorrect fundamentals, their development will reach a point where they are not making progress and they will never reach their true potential.

It would be similar to playing golf and never receiving a lesson from a professional. You may hit the ball where you want it to go on occasion, yet your rounds of golf will be filled with frustration while being stuck in a quagmire of mediocrity, and you still don't know what you don't know. You don't know what you are doing wrong, or for that matter, what you are doing right. If you learn the proper fundamentals of golf, and with consistent practice, you will have the potential to build and improve your skill-set.

That's my analogy for the skill of public speaking—Golf. Without the proper fundamentals, you'll be a hacker for life.

The tagline of this book is "...from someone who actually does it." That's important for you to know, as there are plenty of books on the market sharing public speaking skills, yet the authors of those books are not getting booked and paid to speak from the corporate market. Many people will tell you how to do something, yet they are not doing it themselves.

This book will change the way you speak or present in public, and how you see and hear other speakers. If you take the time to master the simple steps in this book, you will become a solid, influential speaker who can deliver a message and impact the audience in any situation. That is the key...to be able to deliver a quality, impactful message in any situation. It's easy to give a public talk or presentation to people who like you or are supposed to like you (if you are the CEO of your company), yet having the skill level to connect with an audience who doesn't know or care who you are and impact them as human beings...now that's powerful.

After you read this book, you will also look at other speakers differently. You will marvel at how many people are out there speaking or presenting who are not very good. They could be if they made the choice to improve or had the opportunity to learn from an expert, yet they are in a comfortable environment and they receive applause or respect from their audience which leads them to believe they are effective.

This book contains my proven secret formula to a perfect presentation that will assist you to build the proper fundamentals to learn how to deliver a message to an audience the right way and build on your success. You will learn the five-step formula to a perfect presentation along with additional keys to success.

1
MOST OF US ARE NOT CELEBRITIES

This discussion in my mind came into consciousness a few years ago as my wife Jennifer and I were coming back from an oversees business trip. I spoke in five different countries on the topics of Leadership, Communication and Maximizing Your True Potential in life and in business.

As we were close to our boarding time on the 11-hour trip from Copenhagen, Denmark, to JFK, followed by another 5 hours to Vegas, I spotted the "hot-selling" book from Steve Jobs titled **The Presentation Secrets of Steve Jobs: How to Be Insanely Great in Front of Any Audience**. Naturally, I was intrigued. So with a long journey ahead, I bought it.

Being a Steve Jobs fan and a loyal Mac and Apple product user, I enjoyed the book. The information in the book, though often times philosophical and advanced, would help any public speaker deliver a solid talk. Yet the fact is, at the time of the book publishing, Steve Jobs was the most intriguing, brilliant and sought after CEO in the world. With that being said, even IF his presentations were poorly delivered, people would applaud at his brilliance and want to see and hear him speak.

What made Steve Jobs the hottest CEO in the world were obviously the Apple products that were changing the way the world listened to music and communicated. Apple was the hottest product in the world, and Steve Jobs was a celebrity. People weren't excited about Steve Jobs; they were excited about what product Apple was going to launch…and it was awesome. If Steve was the CEO of a company that produced products that weren't "game-changers"—I doubt he would have been deemed a great public speaker. Who is the CEO of Motorola? How about Samsung?

The point here is that YOU are not Steve Jobs, nor am I for that matter. Television personalities, entertainers, athletes, or celebrities don't have to be good speakers or communicators; people want to hear them speak.

We, on the other hand (all of us not signing autographs at restaurants), must be able to execute the proper fundamentals to connect with any audience, deliver an impactful message, teach the audience something, then inspire them to action.

Years ago I did a video shoot for NAPA Auto Parts with Dick Vitale, the ESPN and ABC Basketball analyst. He had been one of my heroes since meeting him years ago while attending a Five-Star basketball camp as a high school basketball player, and then again when he was head coach of the Detroit Pistons. Dick is a passionate guy, and he cares. He told me a story about how he was speaking at a big awards banquet and "was on" before a Hall of Fame baseball player. Of course Dick is a professional. He was prepared, and he knows how to connect and deliver a message to his audience. The Hall of Fame baseball player spoke after Dick and just flopped. He flopped because he came after Dick

Vitale who raised the bar and exposed the Hall of Famer's lack of skills and preparation, which he wasn't accustomed to. The Hall of Famer was used to being loved and applauded during every appearance, yet not this time.

The Hall of Famer didn't have the skills and the proper fundamentals to deliver a solid presentation. I'm going to teach you those skills now.

2
THE UNFAIR ADVANTAGE

People often times ask me how I built my speaking career and how I learned to do what I do— Deliver an effective talk to any audience under any circumstances.

If you ask most speakers how they started their career, you'll hear some interesting stories for sure. Contained in those stories is how they created opportunities to speak and develop their skills. For me, I did just that...created opportunities to speak, and I did it more than most because of my environment.

I found a way to get hired (a great story for another time) in January of 1994 as a field sales representative (FSR) for Robbins Research International (RRI), which was Tony Robbins' company. We were glorified sales reps who were paid on a commission-only basis for selling tickets to Tony's up and coming one-day business seminar. I say "glorified" as we were essentially sales professionals, yet we were selling seminar tickets to the corporate world in a public speaking format. We would perform a "front of the room" presentation as our sales delivery method.

We were labeled as "Tony's top speakers and trainers," and we would speak at weekly corporate sales meetings with the intent to sell the employees of the company tickets to Tony's upcoming one-day live business event.

Like any other sales position, we had "numbers" or quotas we had to hit. In my six years at RRI, I saw a lot of talented people who couldn't hit their numbers and had to find opportunities elsewhere.

Why?

Because delivering a solid, influential message in front of people is difficult. When you're not a celebrity or known public speaker, you must be better than good. It's easy to give a talk when people have come together to hear your message. Yet when your audience was mandated to be there as an employee, there were many obstacles to overcome. The bottom line was you made improvements fast or you were gone.

There were many factors involved. We were often times speaking to an audience that didn't want to hear us speak. Maybe their sales manager brought one of us in to fire up their team, yet the sales team was in disarray, or the company was in disarray for that matter. Often times the manager who brought one of us in as the guest speaker didn't have respect of their team. As a result our talks were met with resistance from our audience. Often times there would be time limitations, interruptions or even attendees who would challenge our expertise.

Nevertheless, we were expected to sell tickets, and to do that, we had to do three things, and we had to do them well.

a. Create a connection (Rapport & Trust)

b. Build Value

c. Inspire them (Inspire them to buy)

Essentially, our mission was to be skilled enough to get past the outer shell or defense mechanisms of the individual audience member. It was our job to find a way to skillfully penetrate their defenses and to connect with their human spirit of achievement and possibility. To open up their minds and hearts, if just only for 30-45 minutes, just enough for them to believe that they could change their results enough to take out their credit cards and give us a commitment.

This was a tough deal, and like anything else, the more we did it, the more effective we became. Let me re-phrase that—the more we did it right, the more effective we became.

It's no secret that perfect practice makes perfect. We learned from the best; there was no question about that. Yet the most valuable piece of this equation was being placed in an environment where I could get quality repetitions everyday and receive immediate feedback

EVERYDAY!

I was giving between two and three presentations per day, six days a week.

That equals:

- 12–18 live presentations per week
- 48–72 per month
- 576–864 per year

I've shared those numbers with other professional speakers I've met over the years, and they all respond in a similar manner – "INCREDIBLE."

I had the opportunity to develop my speaking skills in that unique environment for six years. My last couple of years at RRI, my number of meetings presented was lower, as I was training the other speakers on their craft. In total I performed over 2,500 live talks prior to leaving RRI at the end of 1999 and going out on my own in the year 2000.

My first year at RRI (1994) was an incredible learning experience, with many challenges and a lot of growth. By the second year, I had established myself as one of the best on his team. I continued to elevate my skills and was promoted to the team leader and performed "guest events" for Tony domestically and internationally. I was sent overseas multiple times to teach his international constituents how to master the skills of the "talk" and achieve results.

For me, it was an unfair advantage to be placed in an environment where I could perform "live reps" and get immediate feedback from an unpaid corporate audience. I knew it, and I was committed to taking advantage of my opportunity. Many other FSRs came and went during my time. Some because they couldn't get it done. Others because they felt they were ready to go out on their own and start their own business. My mindset was to immerse myself in the opportunity until I was bulletproof.

Because of the environment, I could use a certain introduction/rapport building technique during an afternoon and experience instant results. If necessary, I would then make changes to my introduction for next morning's meeting. It was a constant adaptation of language patterns, syntax and strategy.

To make the experience even more interesting, I was surrounded by other talented men and women who were also building their skills for the next chapter in their speaking careers. If there was such a thing as a university for public speakers, this was it. People like Niurka Hernandez, Mike Lindstrom, Chuck Douglas, Joe (Skip) Ward, Brett Figueroa, Peter Montoya and Doug Grady. Our sales team was the equivalent of a mastermind group for speaking and influencing.

Niurka is now a best-selling author, speaker and educator in the spiritual transformational world. Mike Lindstrom is respected as the most sought after success coach in the insurance and financial services space. Chuck Douglas is one of the most powerful speakers I've ever seen, and he continues to change lives through speaking and training as well as promoting icons in the industry. Joe (Skip) Ward is now president of success based company out of the New York area. (I learned a lot from Skip. He and I roomed together and competed head to head in my early years. He was magical at creating rapport and connecting to an audience.) Brett Figueroa is a flat out hustler who is passionate about changing lives. He has a successful coaching practice out of Denver, CO. Peter Montoya is the president of Peter Montoya, Inc., an author and a great speaker. Doug Grady, who fantastic speaker and trainer is the president of High Achievers, a professional and personal training and development company based company in Atlanta.

Like any sales team, we would have weekly meetings to talk about the numbers, what was working and who was "hot." In addition, it was common for our team to meet casually at the pool after work and talk about a new technique or method that we were having success with. I was compressing decades of experience into years, and years of experience into months. It was incredible.

As a result, I know HOW to connect with ANY audience and deliver an impactful message, no matter what the situation may be.

Now I'm going to share that with YOU.

3

PSYCHOLOGY

Before I share with you my five-step formula on how to structure your perfect presentation, we must address your psychology. All effective speakers or presenters have their psychology set up to win. They have a belief system that supports them and effectively enables them to convey a message and influence people.

Let me give you an analogy. If you were to walk into your Monday morning corporate meeting and you felt unprepared and, in addition, you didn't have the appropriate materials and you didn't feel confident, how do you think you would perform?

Not very well.

Let's say you were going to a party, and you felt like you didn't have a proper invitation, or you didn't feel good about what you were wearing. How confident would you be?

Not Very

It's the same as a public speaker or anyone giving a live presentation. You must have the right psychology in order to be successful. A superstar speaker's psychology or belief system comes from the experience and the knowing that they can do it.

In the meantime while you build your experience base, here are three beliefs that you can adopt right now to assist you with your psychology.

Belief #1: I may not be a professional, yet I'm real and people appreciate that.

Trust me on this one; being a polished, slick and perfect presenter does not always translate into people buying into what you have to say. People connect to and are influenced by people they like, trust or respect. What is important is for you to be real. If you adopt the belief that you are real and that people appreciate the fact that you are real, you will have more confidence, be more relaxed and your message will come out with clarity.

Belief #2: I have something meaningful to say, and these people want to hear me.

If you really believed that what you had to say was important to your audience and they WANTED to hear you, how relaxed would you be? How confident would you be? This belief gives you a whole different perspective on delivering your message.

You realize that half of the things that you currently believe aren't true anyway...so you might as well believe that your message is important and people want to hear you. I'll help you with the rest!

Belief #3: The energy I give, is the energy I will receive.

Simply put, if you start your talk or presentation with low energy because you lack confidence, your audience feels it, and they return the favor. If you bring energy, your audience will give it back.

The rule of thumb for energy is as follows: As the speaker or presenter, you MUST come in with a higher level of energy than your audience.

Here's what I mean: On an imaginary 0-10 scale for energy levels, 10 is the highest; if your audience is at a level 6, you must come in at a 7 or above. If they are at a 3, then you can come in at a 5 or 6. If they are at an 8, you better bring it! You cannot expect to convey a message and influence others with an energy level that is below the current energy level of your audience.

Watch video on the psychology of a great presenter at http://www.youtube.com/watch?v=sNk_adrLLBo.

4
PRE-GAME

I call this section pre-game because, like an athlete, the presenter or speaker must get "game ready." What does that mean?

All sports are different in pre-game preparation and for that matter, all athletes have different methods to get themselves ready. The same goes for you.

What we prepare is our physiology—our body. Like we talked about in the previous section, you MUST be at a higher energy level than your audience. The easiest, most effective method to raise your energy level is to move your body in a definitive manner. Something out of the ordinary such as jumping jacks, shadow boxing, martial arts kicks, dancing...whatever comes most natural to you.

The point is, you must "walk out on stage" with a strong and confident physiology.

When you think about a person who is confident, we see someone who is:

- Standing tall

- Shoulders back

- Deep breathing

- Eyes up (connecting with audience)

Even today, after thousands of paid speaking events around the world, prior to my talk or presentation, I engage my body in a series of movements, thus instantly increasing my energy level. It's a fundamental for success. I don't skip the fundamentals.

Your first step in your pre-game is to get your body upright, strong and confident, which will automatically increase your energy level.

The second step is you must smile. Smiling is a fundamental that magically allows you to be approachable to your audience. People are attracted to people who are smiling. Smiling presupposes kindness. The challenge is that smiling during a talk is not a natural act. It can be natural if you are telling a light-hearted fun story, yet being able to smile during your talk is a skill that takes practice.

Just to be clear, it's not necessary or productive to have a perma-smile on your face during a talk or presentation, yet having the ability to be present in the moment and smile gives the audience a feeling of connection. People like to be around people who are smiling.

During our Speaker and Presentation Training, I am constantly reminding our participants to smile during their talk. Like anything else, it takes practice. As you develop your skills and have the opportunity to video record yourself, you can see your degree of smiling and where you need to improve. Practice in front of the mirror, and you'll get where you want to go.

You now have two pre-game musts prior to you "going on stage" and giving your talk or presentation:

1. Raise the energy level of your body, stand tall and walk with confidence.

2. Smile

As you know, first impressions happen fast!

5
FIVE STEPS TO A PERFECT PRESENTATION

As I said earlier, being a public speaker that is effective in any situation is difficult. Yet, that's the goal. The goal is to be rock-solid so that no matter what gets thrown at you, you can handle the situation and exceed expectations.

I can teach you all the inside stuff: the secrets, the language patterns, the NLP frames, the personality styles. I can teach it ALL to you…but not today.

My belief is that you must be effective with the fundamentals before you can move on and add new layers of skills. I can and will teach you the advanced skills in the next book, or you can learn in our speakers' training events here in Las Vegas.

Since 2000, when I went out on my own as a speaker, corporate consultant and business coach, I've done an additional 1,000 paid speaking events and traveled the world. Over the last 24 months alone, I've been in 30 counties speaking about success and how to implement strategies in your life and business to achieve results. As an expert in human behavior, I package my message in a manner that allows the audience to make changes in their behavior and increase results.

I'm not a recognized public figure and haven't achieved celebrity status, yet the reason I continue to get hired to speak with companies all over the world, is I deliver results. My message is clear, it's entertaining and it adds value…and most of all, according to clients and re-peat customers, I'm relatable.

In this book, I'm going to teach you the fundamentals that will give you the edge in any speaking situation, and most importantly, teach you the "right" way. When you learn my proven five-step formula "CAMRI" you'll be on the right track for success.

The secret five-step formula to a perfect presentation is not a theory or a concept; it's a formula for success. I've tested, tested and re-tested this formula on live audiences all over the world. Whether you are speaking to executive audiences, mid-level managers, blue-collar audiences, men, women, high-income earners, college students or athletes—I have developed a five-step formula for a perfect presentation that you can use starting today that will deliver positive results for you.

Here it is:

1. Connection
2. Agenda
3. Message
4. Review
5. Inspire

Over the next five chapters you will learn a simple, yet effective outline to follow to help you learn the proper fundamentals of delivering an impactful and effective public speech or presentation.

Whether you are delivering a message to an organization, the parents of your youth sports team, your company or a group of executives, this five-step formula will always deliver results for you.

When you have mastered these five steps, then and only then can I share advanced techniques practiced by only the select few. The select few are the ones who are or have been committed to learning the art of speaking. The celebrity speakers don't know or use this information. Why? Because celebrities and public figures don't have to be effective speakers or good communicators. Remember, if you are signing autographs when you're out for dinner, no one cares if you deliver any value on your talks or presentations. People just want to be around you.

So let's go!

6

THE CONNECTION

The first step in the five-step CAMRI formula is the C—for Connection.

The connection is the most important part of your talk, because without connection, you'll have to work harder to "get" your audience. You've heard the phrase "the speaker had them in the palm of his/her hand." You won't have that experience without having the skill to connect with your audience.

You may be skilled enough to "get" them over the course of your talk, yet if you can "get" them up-front, that's the ticket.

When I say "get" your audience, I'm simply referring to the moment that your audience feels they like you or they can relate with you.

This moment happens when "In the minds of the audience," they are saying to themselves:

- "Yes, me too"
- "I can relate to that"
- "I like him/her"
- "I trust him/her"
- "He/She knows who I am/we are"

The key is simple: We must connect with the audience in the first few minutes and allow them to see who we are, and that we respect them and know who they are.

For the sake of duplication and creating a formula for you to build on, your connection phase is your introduction. It's how you introduce yourself and your topic to the audience.

You build the trust and your relatability by following these steps:

- Being "real"—nobody wants to hear from someone who is so polished and perfect. Sharing how you've learned from others and made mistakes along the way gives others the "me too" connection.

- Smile—Sounds easy, right? A sense of being approachable, even on stage brings a feeling of connection to your audience. Being up on a pedestal may work for the CEO, yet not for an outside speaker coming in to deliver a message.

- Create a "conversation" with the audience—meaning a conversation is more interesting than a presentation. A conversation is interactive. A conversation is a two-way exchange of energy. A presentation is one-way exchange—the presenter talking and the audience listening. How long can you actually listen to someone before your mind starts to drift off to what you need to do next in your day?

- Acknowledging your audience — In simple terms, acknowledging your audience for their achievements, their hard work, sacrifice or productivity. You could even recognize the challenges of the current marketplace, constant change or new obstacles awaiting them.

- Share with the audience who you are and what qualifies you to speak in front of them today.

Every speaking situation stands alone and is individual by nature. You will experience different audiences with unique circumstances. As a result, I will give you a simple delivery you can mold into your specialized situation.

Being Real: This is a state of being rather than a decision. If you are not real, it's difficult to turn on the switch to be real. Here is the distinction: when speaking to an audience, the key is to connect with them. If a speaker comes off as perfectly polished or accomplished with no blemishes, the speaker is not relatable to the audience. Being real and vulnerable is a quality that takes a speaker from good to great.

Someone asked me once what I meant by being real. The best way I can explain it, is when you are having a heart-to-heart conversation with your friend, your child or a relative. Allowing yourself to be in that openhearted place during your presentation will give you the edge and allow you to connect with any audience at any time.

One memorable moment at RRI, was when Tony Robbins called on me to perform a 10-minute product sales piece at his one-day business event in New York City on the spur of the moment. This is where he sets up the opportunity for product sales prior to the lunch break, and then walks off stage for someone else to explain and sell the products, <u>which he had never done before</u>. There were 7,000 people attending and the place was rocking. The challenge was that I wasn't aware he wanted me to do it until his assistant informed me only one hour prior to when I was supposed to be on stage! We had not reviewed the products or had I ever practiced what he was asking me to do on his biggest stage. He had confidence in me, so of course I said yes. Long story short, I could have done better. Later that night during our debrief, he shared with me a lesson about being real. When you feel things aren't going well, it's okay to be human and drop the sales script and just come from the heart. It was a big lesson for me. A lesson that gave me the first hand experience of what it meant to be real and connect with the audience in a tough situation.

<u>Smile</u>: Easy enough. Just do it. Some people have to practice this step, as smiling while giving a presentation is natural for some and uncomfortable for others. Practice in front of a mirror. Record yourself. People enjoy watching

and listening to someone who is smiling and having a good time rather than being serious, too corporate or uptight.

<u>Create a conversation</u>: Again, there are many methods to do this, yet I establish the fact that I am having a conversation with my audience up front. However I decide to greet my audience…"good morning, good afternoon or good evening," I'm looking to get a response back from them, which of course doesn't happen all of the time. My experience says only 10 percent of any audience will respond because of their corporate culture or situation. That means 90 percent of the audience members don't respond.

When a speaker just starts in on the presentation after saying good morning and receiving nothing back from the audience, the speaker has just told the audience that they are irrelevant—this is my talk, so just listen up. If you were sitting down at a Starbucks with a potential business client and you said "hello" and they didn't reciprocate, and you just started talking about you or your product and what you can do for them, that would be awkward to say the least.

When you address your audience and they don't respond, it's a great time to pause and re-package the statement, put some additional energy in the statement along with some exaggerated gestures.

For instance...Good morning ABC company. (Cricket, cricket). This is the ABC company right? This is the group that just posted incredible second quarter numbers? Let's try it again...Good Morning! (While raising the voice tone a bit and extending both arms out to the audience)

They will ALWAYS respond with a solid "Good Morning." You're off to a good start.

By using the above strategy, the audience knows that you are on top of your game. You're not just some speaker with a canned talk. You are confident and have something important to share.

Remember, you are in control of the room. You set the tone for the talk. If you are passive and not in control of the room, the audience can feel it. If you are confident and in control, the audience knows it.

Let's be clear about situational talks; if you were to get introduced as part of a casual meeting or event, maybe a "hello, good afternoon, or good evening" is not necessary. That's for you to decide. My coaching is when in doubt, do it. It's always good to establish yourself and a confident speaker that is present. Present being the key!

<u>Acknowledging Your Audience</u>: Everybody wants to feel recognized. Everyone wants to feel like they are appreciated. As a speaker, it's your job to know your audience—who they are, what they have accomplished, what they are going through, etc.

In my speaker training sessions, we cover the nine keys a speaker must know prior to the talk. Knowing your audience is one of those keys.

For the sake of this example, let's say you are speaking to a group of sales professionals who had a tough year last year filled with changes and challenges. The meeting is a kick-off for the upcoming year.

Here's an example of an acknowledgement piece in your connection formula:

"I'm excited to be here today...it's always great when I have the opportunity to meet with a group of people who are fighters, who understand that accomplishing amazing things never comes easy, yet are ready for the challenge. I know all of you fought through a challenging year last year and are excited to start this year and come out of the gates strong!"

Obviously every situation is different, and making them feel like you know what they have been though will allow you as a speaker to get one step closer to creating the connection.

If you were speaking in front of a group of professional women in the corporate world:

"As I was preparing for our meeting today, I thought about the women in this room and the amount of respect I have for all of you. Besides being successful females in the corporate world, which is admirable on its own, many of you are mothers and wives, balancing the non-stop demands of raising a family along with success in the corporate world. Some of you are single mothers and providing both love and leadership for your family. For a time in my life, I was raised by a single mother, and I know first hand the challenges that come along with that opportunity. So I want to let all of you know before we get started today, that I am honored to be here today with you and I appreciate the opportunity to share."

Again, the goal is to recognize the audience for "who they are" in their life. You could recognize the group for their accomplishments, yet people really love to be acknowledged for their character. Think about when someone tells you that you are a fighter, or you're honest, hard working and have a never-say-die attitude. It makes you feel good. People like to listen to people who appreciate them. So do a bit of homework about your audience and make certain you acknowledge them in your connection piece.

<u>Share who you are and what gives you the opportunity to speak in front of them today</u>: Essentially, who are you and what have you done to give you the right to speak with the audience today.

For myself, I speak on success. I am an expert on human behavior, and I package my message into specific keys to success and how the audience can take steps today to make improvements. My success principles apply to sales, leadership, communication, life success, or corporate culture.

Sharing with the audience what gives you the "right" to speak with them today is a tricky proposition. You want to establish yourself as an expert, yet you don't want to be pompous or arrogant.

Rather than saying how great I am or all I have accomplished, I want to share with my audience how blessed I have been over the last 20 years to work with some of the most talented mentors and most respected leaders in the world. In addition, I include my amazing clients and the top performers I have had the opportunity to coach and learn from.

With that in mind, my connection chunk on who am I could go something like this:

"Over the past 20 years, I've been blessed to have worked along with and learned from the top life and business advisors in the world: Brian Tracy, Denis Waitley, Og Mandino, and Tony Robbins. I've had the honor to learn from the hundreds and hundreds of clients of mine who are great leaders, sales performers, marketing strategists, entrepreneurs, and mothers and fathers. Over the past 24 months, I've been in over 30 countries sharing my knowledge with high achievers just like you who are looking for edge to be the best they can be."

Remember, people want to know what your qualifications are. "What gives you the right to speak to us?" If they had a chance to ask you they would, and you are the speaker, so the key is to answer the question for them and put their unconscious mind to rest.

7

AGENDA

Again, I am sharing with the proper fundamentals for you to master a success formula for pubic speaking thus allowing your skill level to grow. You have completed step one in the five steps to a perfect presentation—Connection.

Step two in the CAMRI success formula is your Agenda.

    C—Connection

    A—Agenda

The agenda simply means, where are you going?

A simple analogy that will make it clear for you why stating your agenda is a must, and how many average and below average speakers, famous or not, miss the mark on this one.

If I called you on the phone and said—"Hey, I'm coming over to your house in 1 hour and I'm picking you up."

What are some questions that you may be asking? How about, where are we going? How long will we be gone? Are we having dinner? What would be the appropriate attire? Do I need to bring a change of clothes? You get the idea. It would be unreasonable for anyone to call you on the phone and tell you they are coming by to pick you up in an hour with no explanation for what you will be doing or where you will be going.

To add another layer of complexity to this step, when people are listening to a speaker speak, they are drifting in and out of being present. They are drifting in and out of consciousness. That's just how human beings are wired. As a listener, we may be focused at the beginning of the talk, yet then something is said and it causes us to think about something else in our life, which causes us to loose our presence in the talk.

As a speaker or presenter, you want to take any questions that the audience could be asking out of the equation during your introduction. I've found the best time to do this is during the agenda.

An example of a poor agenda: "Today I'm going to share with you how to increase your market presence using social media."

Every audience member will ask one if not all of the following questions in their mind:

- How long is he/she going to be talking
- Are they going to talk about Pinterest?
- How about Tumblr?
- I wonder how he/she feels about Instragram?
- Is Facebook overrated?

When the audience is asking themselves questions about the content or the length of the talk, they are not listening to YOU, thus they are not with you, connecting with you, or even hearing you.

A solid example of the agenda part of your introduction would be as follows:

"Today we are going to talk about increasing your market presence using social media, so over the next 30 minutes, I'm going to share with you three strategies you can start using today to increase your social media presence using Facebook, Twitter and YouTube."

Can you notice the difference?

It's clear, it's concise and it's structured. The audience knows what you are talking about, how long you are talking and how many points you have.

Great speakers or presenters have an agenda. Amateurs don't.

Again, just because someone may be naturally dynamic or charismatic, that doesn't make them an effective speaker. They may think they are; as a matter of fact, I'm sure they think they are. However, the real gauge of an effective speaker is what your audience remembers or applies to their life or business after you complete your talk or presentation.

As you listen to speakers in the future, listen for their agenda and use both the good ones, and the not so good ones, to assist you in becoming a master at laying your talk out for your audience and therefore taking away their natural questions.

Visit http://www.youtube.com/watch?v=VZmS4A2uPUc to see video on Agenda.

8
YOUR MESSAGE

You now have two crucial secrets of the five steps to a perfect presentation—Connection and Agenda.

Your message is the third step in organizing a perfect presentation. Again, we are building the proper fundamentals so you can refine and improve with each and every speech or presentation.

1. C—Connection

2. A—Agenda

3. M—Your Message

The message is simply the body of your talk. What specifically are you talking about? In your agenda you indicated the title of your talk, which was Increasing Your Social Presence Using Social Networking. In addition, you indicated that you were going to share three strategies using Facebook, Twitter and YouTube.

Your message, also known as the body of your talk, (Increasing your market presence using social media), would be organized into three points based on the agenda we created in step two: Facebook, Twitter and YouTube.

As you start your talk, the next step is a simple transition to strategy number 1—Facebook. For instance, your language may be as simple as: "So the first strategy to increase market presence using social media is Facebook."

Now you are into the first point or strategy of your message.

If you are using a PowerPoint or Prezi delivery system, here are a few things to remember:

1. People get bored with numbers and data. You want people to remember you and your talk for being impactful not boring. Data, stats or facts are ok, yet use them to support points, not to read through slide after slide.

2. A PowerPoint or Prezi should be used as a support to your talk, not as the talk. Reading from one slide to the next to your audience is unacceptable.

3. Use bullet points or images with text to transition you to the next point. What I mean here is that your presentation is something you should be able to talk about confidently and calmly. You should be able to talk about your message over dinner or at a bar. With that in mind, the PowerPoint is simply a visual aid for both you and the audience.

Moving on to the fundamentals for the message. Your message should be assembled in the following manner:

1. Statement/Facts

2. Supporting Story

3. Education/How?

For example, in one of my most popular talks titled Maximize Your True Potential, one of my agenda points or message points, is ATTITUDE.

In my talk, I transition into my next agenda point by saying, "Strategy (or Point) number two is Attitude." As indicated above, my message starts out with statements or facts about Attitude.

1. Facts/Statements

"Ladies and Gentlemen, attitude is the little thing that makes the big difference in your performance. I love talking about attitude because it's one of the only things that you and I can control each and every day. We are not able to control the stock market, the interest rates or the weather, yet every day you and I can wake up in the morning, put our feet on the floor and make a decision to have a winning attitude."

Obviously this is abbreviated, yet you get the point. Whatever statements, facts, headlines, quotes, or opinions you have should be laid out in the first section of your message.

2. Story

People remember stories. You know the old saying, facts tell—stories sell. It's true. People lose interest in facts, statements and numbers, yet they are attracted to stories. Stories are trance inducers, meaning people naturally engage in stories, and lose the sense of time.

Human behavior indicates that when listening to a presenter or speaker, the human mind drifts in and out of consciousness based on how the messaging is packaged. When people hear stories, they stay conscious to the story and actually feel the experience.

As a presenter, you have three types of stories you
can tell:

A. Stories about yourself

B. Stories about someone notable, i.e., a celebrity or someone who has accomplished something of interest.

C. Third Party Stories. Third party stories are stories about someone else, yet the language patterns used shift as if you are talking directly to your audience. This strategy is incredibly powerful. The third party story strategy is not a fundamental skill. It's an advanced skill, so I'm not teaching it in this book. We teach it in our live Presentation Skills training, and it will also be in my follow-up book, so stay tuned.

Moving on with the example of my message on attitude from my talk titled Maximize your

True Potential, I started out with some facts/statements—

"Ladies and Gentlemen, attitude is the little thing that makes the big difference in your performance. I love talking about attitude because it's one of the only things that you and I can control each and every day. We're not able to control the stock market, the interest rates or the weather, yet everyday you and I can wake up in the morning, put our feet on the floor and make a decision to have a winning attitude."

Then, transition into a story:

"Years ago when I first started out in this business, I was hired to do a motivational keynote for a fortune 200 company out of Chicago. I was kicking off the meeting following a short message from the CEO. I was a bit nervous, so I thought I would make my way around the room prior the to the talk and meet a few people. There were 300 people set up in theatre style, similar to our room today. There was a stage up front and of course from my perspective, a right section, a middle section and a left section. So I went down to the right section about 10 minutes prior to the CEO's talk and walked up to a guy and said, Hi, I'm Dan Lier. I'll be speaking today after your CEO…how are you doing. He responded with…"

I'm into the story, and people are engaged. The purpose of my story is related to one of my agenda points—the importance of having a winning attitude and how not having a winning attitude will limit your career advancement.

As a presenter, it's great if you can layer multiple stories on top of each other. The stories should be short, anywhere from 2 to 10 minutes in length. Any story longer than 2 to 10 minutes is unnecessary and it's risky. Risky in the fact that if you're not a great storyteller or the story is not as good as you think it is, you will lose your audience.

Your goal is to keep your audience engaged! On occasion, speakers and presenters get long-winded and it becomes more about them than about the message or teaching the audience something. Unfortunately, it's common to hear average or overrated speakers tell long stories either about their accomplishments or their experiences, which may be entertaining (depending on the status of the speaker or their skill level), yet what people really want is the HOW. How can I apply this to my life or my business?

This is the part three of your message: The Education or The HOW

In my example of the my talk Maximize Your True Potential with the agenda point of Attitude, after I share my stories, it's time to share with my audience HOW to make changes in their life. Depending on the allotted time, I would then share anywhere from three to five tools on HOW to have or maintain a winning attitude. Educate! This is a key to your success. You don't have to have three to five tools on "how"—one will suffice. Yet, you need to have at least one.

Visit http://www.youtube.com/watch?v=qAv7qylzNBY to see video example of one of my HOW's for changing your attitude and the way people see you.

In the world of corporate speaking, you will hear the phrase "the take-away." The take-away is a term used to pinpoint what the audience is going to "take away" or learn from the meeting. From my perspective, sharing with an audience that having a winning attitude is a must, not a take-away. The take-away is "How" can they turn their attitude around when things are not going well, or "what" can they do today to change the way in which they process the events or happenings in their world—which leads to a winning attitude.

Companies want ROI—Return on Investment

I've been blessed to create a name for myself in the corporate world as an expert in human behavior and peak performance, so I consistently get booked for paid speaking engagements. From the feedback that I have received from my clients, there are three specific reasons that I have been successful in this area:

1. I'm relatable

2. I'm good at what I do

3. ROI—I provide skills for the audience to apply to their business and their life.

Dynamic content and education is in—FLUFF is OUT. You can be fluffy if you are a celebrity. If you're not, you better bring some content.

Let's continue with our hypothetical talk, which is titled "Increasing Your Social Presence Using Social Networking." In your agenda, you indicated that you were going to share three strategies using Facebook, Twitter and YouTube.

Your message, or the body of your talk, would be organized into three points: Facebook, Twitter and YouTube. As you start your talk, it's simply a transition to strategy number one—Facebook.

As you've just learned, the proper method of assembling a solid message consists of three parts: The Statement/Facts, Stories and Education.

It would be easy to talk about Facebook facts. Over a billion users, etc., followed by a story about how a restaurant or other business not only increase their social presence by using Facebook, but increased their lunch revenues by 10 percent.

No kidding. We've all heard those facts and stories before, and we will continue to hear them. What will separate you from the rest is sharing with the audience what they can do TODAY to help them get the same results. I'm stressing the word TODAY, because it's one thing to start sharing technical strategies that "go over" most of the audiences heads, yet it's another to give them do-able action steps that they can apply now. When your audience walks away excited and saying to themselves, "I can do this"...you have become an effective communicator.

I spoke just last week at a kick-off event for the MAGIC show, which is a massive apparel show in Las Vegas. I spoke after a presentation by another speaker who was talking about social media. The speaker specializing in social media gave facts and figures, yet the people in the audience were not inspired to go set up a LinkedIn account or start using Twitter. They didn't have the steps and actions for TODAY. The message was conceptual rather than achievable. A sleeper. Big Difference.

9
REVIEW

C—Connection

A—Agenda

M—Message

R—Review

The review is a simple summary of what you just talked about. You are sharing with your audience what you just shared with them. As speakers and presenters, we've all heard that before, yet many don't do it.

Remember, people go in and out of consciousness during any presentation or talk. They could have some personal issues at home, with their kids or even a potential business deal that is consuming their mind space, which is not unusual or uncommon.

It's not that your talk wasn't entertaining or exciting, it's just that as humans, our minds wander. As an expert communicator, presenter or speaker, it's your job to make sure you fill in the gaps at the end with a quick summary.

The transition phrase that has been effective for me is simply, "in review."

"In review we talked about the three strategies you must implement to Maximize Your True Potential." Then, I give a quick summary. A summary is just that—a summary, not another presentation.

For example, on my second agenda point Attitude, I would say something to this effect:

"...then we talked about the importance of having a winning attitude and that YOU are in charge or your attitude, and it's your choice of what type of attitude that you have. We talked about the greeting strategy, your baggage and how to change the questions you ask yourself that affect your attitude."

This would be an example of one of my agenda points. It's quick. It's to the point, yet it reminds them of the message and what they learned.

The Review step is a valuable fundamental for two reasons:

First of all, it allows you to "package" and present your message points to your audience reminding them of the points of your talk. I like to think of it as "packaging my talk" as if it were a present to my audience. The vision in my mind is wrapping a present, then putting on a bow and giving it to my audience. My present consists of a nicely wrapped message, which is the message of my talk, and presented to my audience in a manner that they can easily enjoy.

Secondly, people like to feel smart. When you review the points of your message, it's fresh on the mind of your audience. They can, and will walk out of the room and share with people the "three strategies" they learned. Everyone likes to be reminded, and the review step in your five steps to a perfect presentation is a secret to being effective.

10

INSPIRE/CALL TO ACTION

C—Connection
A—Agenda
M—Message
R—Review
I—Inspire

The fifth and final piece to your perfect presentation model is "I" for Inspire. This is where you close out your talk and have what is called a "Call to Action." A "Call to Action" is simply asking yourself, "what do I want my audience to do when I complete my talk?" The answer to your question would be different depending on the context of your talk, your audience and the situation.

In my earlier years when I was out building my presentation skills selling seminar tickets, my only outcome was to influence my audience to buy tickets. That was it. It was interesting to see the new FSRs (Field Sales Reps) when they came out and joined the team; they would go through a phase where initially they just wanted to be liked. All the members of our sales team would see each other in the evenings, and it would be common to ask one another "So, how did your meetings go today?" The new FSRs would often respond by saying something to the effect of, "Oh, my meetings went great. They really liked it." One of the veterans would respond with "how many tickets did you sell?" Because for the seasoned FSRs, we had been through that phase of wanting to be liked or respected, then of course as we matured and our skill level grew, our questions changed. The only thing that mattered was if they bought a ticket or not. Buying a ticket or not depended on if we had connection, built enough value and had an effective close.

Currently my "call to action" is totally different. Most of my talks are private corporate events, which means I have been hired by a company to elevate the performance of their sales, management or leadership teams. With that in mind my INSPIRATION piece or Call to Action is inspiring them to apply the tools I shared with them to their life and their business. My goal is to help the participants take away the self-imposed barriers of what's possible for them and provide the tools they need to perform at a higher level.

Here is an example of what my "I—Inspire" piece may sound like:

"Ladies and Gentlemen, you've been a tremendous audience and here's what I want you to know...that all of you in this room here today are highly skilled, and have exactly what you need to reach and exceed your goals...or you wouldn't be sitting here right now. You have the experience, the know-how, and you are with a company that understands the value of investing in their people. If you make a decision right now and apply just one of these principles that I've shared with you here today, your life and your career will reach new heights...it will never be the same. Yet you have to do it, not talk about it...you have to do it. *So by a show of hands, how many people in here today are committed to applying just one of the strategies you learned today to your life or your business?"

*(You, the speaker raise your hand—and of course everyone raises their hand.)

"(Pause) That's fantastic and I'm excited for you. I hope you enjoyed my talk today, and I wish all of you tremendous success. Thank you! "

* Audience engagements techniques in next book

If you are speaking to a group of parents and you want them to volunteer for a fundraiser, then of course your talk is about the value of the fundraiser and your "I—Inspire" piece may be raising their hand to receive a commitment sheet, or maybe your goal is to get them to get up and go to the table at the back of the room to sign up.

Like I said, every "Call to Action" is different, depending on whom you are talking to and why you are talking to them, yet you still must have the Inspiration piece (step five). People want to know what to do. It's a person's natural tendency to move into action, therefore, they need to know what to do. Every sales manager should have action steps at the end of their talk. Every coach should have the "what do we do now" steps for their team. Make sure you have step five, the Inspire piece, at the end of every one of your talks.

11

BUILDING YOUR SKILLS

You now have the five fundamental pieces for a perfect presentation.

C—Connection
A—Agenda
M—Message
R—Review
I—Inspire

Yes of course, there are many more advanced skills, such as NLP pre-frames for hecklers, know-it-alls or hostile audiences. In addition, I teach anchoring, audience participation strategies, test close strategies, third-party stories, trance inducing statements, and even embedded commands. All of these skills would be considered "the Next Level" and quite frankly, not too many speakers are skilled in these areas or do them well. The good news is that I will teach all of these skills to you in my follow-up book, yet in order to use them, you MUST be solid with your fundamentals. You must be fundamentally sound before you can implement advanced skills and be effective.

It would be similar to a basketball player attempting to dribble behind their back before they have mastered controlled dribbling in all situations—the fast break, under pressure or breaking the press. We must build the foundation before we build the house. Many speakers have built foundations; however, their foundations are faulty. Unfortunately, they didn't learn from a seasoned professional, so they have been presenting over and over again with improper fundamentals. Imagine playing golf for a couple years and no one ever showing you the proper grip. The grip you started with is all you know, so you just keep building on top of an improper fundamental.

The same principal applies to your speaking skills. Always:

- Learn from someone who has done it.

- Learn the proper fundamentals.

- Practice, Practice, Practice

Build your skill-set to where you can apply the five-steps to a perfect presentation to any of your talks in any situation. If you use these five steps, you will improve each and every month. The key is to practice. You must put yourself in a position to work on your skills consistently in order to build your fundamentals. Speaking once per month is not going to allow you to build on your success or your failures, so you must commit to getting reps.

One of the questions I hear from up and coming speakers or people who would like to speak for a living is, "How do I get in front of people and practice?" That's a valid question.

Obviously if you are in a corporate situation where you lead a team of people, this is an easy proposition. You have the ability to assemble at least one new talk each and every week. Most companies have weekly meetings, so you can insert yourself and work on your skills while adding value to your team. If you're in a corporate leadership position and you are not having weekly meetings, it's time for you to start.

If you are not in a corporate leadership position, you can join a speaking club or group such as Toastmasters. In my first corporate position fresh out of college, I was required to join Toastmasters. It was a long time ago, yet I believe we met at least once, maybe twice a month. Toastmasters is fantastic because it allows you to get live reps in a safe environment. Everyone is there for the same reason, so it's a great place to start. As much as I think Toastmasters is a solid place to start, there is a downside as well. Because everyone is there for the same reason and it's a safe environment, everyone is very supportive, which can lead to a false sense of two things: your skill level and what a corporate or non-toastmasters audience is really like.

I've seen that situation over the years many times; a seasoned Toastmaster who struggles in a real environment. Just last year Big O Tires held a two-day franchise owners' event here in Las Vegas and they hired two speakers. I was one of the hired speakers, and the other speaker had a title of a World Champion of Public Speaking. What that meant was, he was the World Champion of the Toastmasters public speaking contest. A contest judged by worldwide Toastmaster members. An environment where the audience comes in smiling, they are responsive and they applaud. In order to win the title of World Champion, there's no doubt that you have to be a solid speaker. Yet, when those skills are taken out into the corporate environment where audience members do not automatically like you, or even want to be there, it's not a smooth transition.

I was keynote speaker on the first day of the Big O Tires franchise owners' event and I delivered a powerful one-hour talk using my five steps to a perfect presentation outline. Subsequently, the attendees rushed to the back of the room, and we sold out of my books and CDs. During my presentation the audience learned specific strategies to apply to their franchises to raise the level of their performance and how to connect more effectively with their customers. My job was successfully done.

The speakers' bureau that booked me received raved reviews on the content of my talk, and how the audience really connected with me. As a speaker, you know if the audience connects with you by the number of people who either buy your books or CDs from the back of the room, or from how many people want to talk with you or shake your hand after the event.

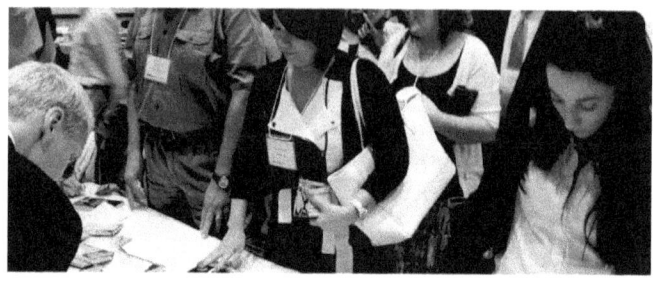

Post Event Book & CD Sales

On the second day of the Big O Tires franchisee event, the other speaker, who was "The World Champion" struggled and received mediocre reviews. My bureau indicated that the second-day speaker didn't connect with the audience and didn't bring any value to the franchise owners. Again, in the right environment, I'm sure the second-day speaker is solid, yet in a world where the speaker has to connect and bring value, he struggled.

Just be clear, I believe that if you haven't been a member of Toastmasters, you should join immediately. You will receive the reps to progress as a speaker and presenter. In addition, you will learn how to think and speak "on the spot." Just keep in mind that in order to get to the next level, you must speak to the public in a "non-secure" environment. (More to come on how to do just that)

When I worked with Tony Robbins' company, which was called Robbins Research International at the time, I would see similar situations. Like I mentioned earlier, along with many other talented people, I was a FSR (Field Sales Rep) and we were paid on commission to sell tickets to attend a Tony Robbins event. We sold those tickets at corporate meetings all over the country; real estate, auto sales, mortgage...any company who had a sales force, they were our targets. Every person on the FSR team had the skills to walk into any company, build rapport, build value, and influence an audience in a corporate meeting type format.

On the inside of the Robbins organization were individuals who spoke specifically to the volunteer staff who worked at Tony's events. If you haven't been to see Tony Robbins live, I suggest you do it when the opportunity arises. The events are big productions, not just your average "sit and learn" seminar environment. As a result, he has hundreds of volunteers who "crew" the events. To train his volunteer crew, he has internal staff members, who are called the leadership team (also unpaid), who perform leadership training to the crew. They get to speak to hundreds of people and teach Tony's material. It's a cool gig, and the people who do it just love it. The challenge is the skills of speaking in a "primed" and safe environment do not translate into success outside of the cocoon.

For a two-year period, the Robbins organization was performing what were called "guest events" where a "guest speaker" from Robbins' would teach and share success strategies and then sell a weekend seminar. The guest events were 2 hours, which entailed 90 minutes of content and approximately 30 minutes to sell the program. The attendees of the event were invited as "special guests," and there was no charge to attend. The numbers of attendees ranged from 400 to 900 people. The most memorable "guest event" I ever led was at the Marriott World Trade Center. The room was set for 700 and 900 people showed up. It was incredible. So in the "guest event" there would be some Robbins fans, of course, along with some curious people, some skeptical people and some people who showed up with a friend and didn't know what was going on.

The bottom line was, if you didn't have the skills necessary to connect and influence an audience that didn't pay to see you or didn't know who you were, you were in trouble. And that's exactly what happened to the members of the leadership team who were unskilled as speakers outside of the cocoon. It was tough because they were friends of mine and seeing them struggle was actually painful.

The corporate office had multiple events going on during the course of a month, so they tested different people in different markets. For instance, I may have been speaking in front of 400 people in one location in Chicago on Wednesday night, and someone else would be speaking to a group of 400 on Thursday night. The corporate office used a few select FSRs and a few select people from the leadership team to speak at the guest events. We would actually attend each other's event to watch and learn from. The leadership team struggled because they were not in an environment where people started clapping when you said "Good evening." Many of the attendees of the guest events had never attended a Tony Robbins' event, or for that matter, ever been exposed to his work. The environment wasn't safe, and it was an eye opener for those who didn't have the street experience.

You must get experience from neutral audiences, and I'm going to share with you how to do it.

Most sales based companies have weekly meetings. Auto dealers, real estate agents, mortgage brokers and insurance agencies would be a great place to start. For their weekly meetings, the sales managers are always looking for a qualified guest speaker to add something new to their meetings. The managers get tired of presenting every week to the sales team, and the sales people get tired of hearing the manager, so it's a great opportunity to hone your skills.

Put yourself a quick promo reel together. With the technology available, such as iMovie or Final Cut, you can assemble a solid reel for a minimal investment.

You can book yourself as a Peak Performance speaker and you will a give a 15-30 minute meeting for them at no-charge...just the opportunity to sell your book at the end. Many of you are saying, "well, that's great, yet I don't have a book."

If you don't, you have two choices: Write one or utilize someone else's book that you believe in. If you haven't written a book, we have a consulting service where you can take any book that you want and brand it for yourself and make it an extension of you. You can read more about that service going to my site.

Lastly, you can practice on your family. There were many times that my kids were tasked to sit and listen to me give a short talk every night. It was challenging, and it was fun. The bottom line is that I was getting reps, and that is one of the keys to success as a speaker. Reps—doing it the right way!

Thank you for investing in yourself and purchasing my book. I'm honored that I can play a part in your development as a speaker and as a person.

Keep Believing and stay ON FIRE!

Dan

Visit http://www.danlier.com/contact-dan to book Dan Lier for:

- Kick-Off Meetings
- Conventions
- Events
- Public Speaking/Presentation Training
- Leadership Training
- Executive Coaching
- Custom Made MP3s

www.DanLier.com

ABOUT THE AUTHOR

Dan Lier is an expert in Human behavior, international speaker and author who earned a Division I college basketball scholarship from the University of Toledo where they were co-MAC champions and earned an NIT birth where they lost to Michigan in the second round. Dan then transferred to Pensacola Junior College for his sophomore year, before attending Fort Hays State University where his college basketball team won two successive national championships. Dan went on to earn his masters' degree while coaching two years of college basketball. While playing basketball at Fort Hays State, where they were ranked #1 in the nation, he met with psychologists about the mental side of performance, which spurred his interest in human behavior.

Dan worked with RRI (Robbins Research International) for six years where he continued his study of human behavior while elevating his public speaking and presentation skills. Dan performed over 2,500 customized live presentations while at RRI, prior to starting his own business in 2000.

Dan is known as "America's Coach" on HSN (Home Shopping Network) where he shared his uniquely formatted "10-Minute Coach" CD programs for millions of viewers for a 2-year period. He followed with his book Titled "The 10 Minute Coach – Daily Strategies for Life Success" published by Beaufort Books in New York.

Dan joined the elite faculty at TSTN (The Success and Training Network) with leaders such as Brian Tracy, Les Brown, Zig Ziglar and Denis Waitley where he created 30-minute TV shows designed for individual and corporate success via subscription. You can see more about TSTN at http://www.tstn.com/your-true-potential-dan-lier/#more-81.

Dan expanded his understanding of human behavior with his second book titled "MEN – 10 Secrets Every Woman Should Know from Two Guys that Do." Dan and co-author Mike Lindstrom traveled around the country performing live events for both men and women and the tendencies of human behavior in relationships.

Dan co-developed a behavior assessment for relationships used around the country by numerous relationship-focused companies to assist couples in relationships to communicate more effectively.

Dan's work on human behavior has been covered by The Today Show, Inside Edition and has been a guest on The Howard Stern show and the O'Reilly Factor, along with countless national radio and regional TV appearances.

Dan Lier continues to book speaking engagements for corporate meetings and conventions around the world. His charismatic delivery style along with his high quality content provide companies with the tools to increase performance. When companies look for a speaker to deliver a powerful message that delivers ROI, they chose Dan. Over the past 24 months, Dan has spoken in over 30 countries on success, achievement, leadership, communication, and how to maximize your true potential.

Dan Lives in Las Vegas, Nevada, with his wife Jennifer and his two children.

www.ingramcontent.com/pod-product-compliance
Lightning Source LLC
Chambersburg PA
CBHW071606170526
45166CB00003B/1005